THE BIBLE,
THE CHURCH,
AND SOCIAL JUSTICE

Richard Schiblin, C.SS.R.

LIGUORI
PUBLICATIONS

One Liguori Drive
Liguori, Missouri 63057
(314) 464-2500

Imprimi Potest:
John F. Dowd, C.SS.R.
Provincial, St. Louis Province
Redemptorist Fathers

Imprimatur:
Monsignor Edward J. O'Donnell
Vicar General, Archdiocese of St. Louis

ISBN 0-89243-187-3

Cover Design by Pam Hummelsheim
Cover Art by Rita Corbin

TABLE OF CONTENTS

Foreword

Good, inexpensive "handbooks" on what the Bible and the Church say about social justice are hard to come by. A booklet like this one is therefore a valuable contribution to education for justice and peace. The author — Father Richard Schiblin, director of House on the Way, in Oakland, California — focuses on five key areas involving faith and justice.

Chapter 1 offers a clear synopsis of what the Bible — the Old and the New Testament — tells us about God's desire for justice on this earth.

Chapter 2 paints a stark picture of poverty in the United States. It then reflects on this situation in terms of Christian faith.

Chapter 3 describes the extreme poverty in Latin America, and outlines structural causes. It tells of the "awakening" of Latin Americans to their plight and tells of their faith-response.

Chapter 4 gives a profile of "basic Christian communities," in which Latin America's poor are banding together in their struggle for justice. The chapter tells how these grassroots communities challenge oppressive institutions, and it traces their lineage to the New Testament.

Chapter 5 brings us back, in a sense, to chapter 1. This final chapter outlines the consistent teaching of modern popes — especially Paul VI and John Paul II. It spells out the biblically based teaching of the Church, which calls upon our two dominant economic systems — capitalism and communism — to become instruments of justice for the people.

The fact that this booklet offers helps for discussion, further study, and concrete social action adds to its worth as a tool for Christian education and involvement.

Liguori Publications is proud to present *The Bible, the Church, and Social Justice* to that ever-growing number of people who "hunger and thirst to see right prevail" (Matthew 5:6).

Daniel L. Lowery, C.SS.R.
Director of Publications

1
The Bible and Justice

A recent letter to the local Catholic paper echoed a sentiment that is heard often these days. Referring to a priest who had withheld his taxes to protest the nuclear arms buildup, the letter said: "Father X is a dangerous man. (His) selfish, publicity-seeking, treasonous rantings endanger (the Church's) work."

Just a week before that, another priest had spoken in a nearby parish about El Salvador. The responses to his talk ranged from a grudging, "Well, I guess we got to hear that stuff" to other far more defiant remarks. One man made a scene of walking out in the middle of the sermon. Another went straight to the pastor after Mass and demanded to be taken off the parish rolls. A third accused the pastor of letting "that priest" come in and promote Communism.

These attitudes reflect a growing tension within the Church. As some feel moved in faith to address issues of justice and peace, others feel that religion should "stay out of politics." Despite this, however, there are strong biblical arguments for the Church's involvement in matters of justice. This chapter will attempt a brief outline of these biblical themes.

Old Testament History

The central event of Old Testament history was the deliverance of the Jewish people from slavery in Egypt. The sight of his people enslaved was painful to Yahweh. " . . . I have indeed seen the misery of my people in Egypt. I have heard their outcry against their slave-masters. I have taken heed of their sufferings and have come down to rescue them . . . " (Exodus 3:7-8). Yahweh's grief is embodied in the cry which Moses addressed, in his name, to Pharaoh. It is a cry which has been echoed by other enslaved peoples throughout history: *"Let my people go!"*

The Lord commanded his people to remember this Exodus event, their deliverance from slavery in Egypt, for the rest of their lives. It was an event that they should celebrate each year, one that would define them as a people. They were a people set free.

When Yahweh established the people in their own land, they were no longer slaves but a free people. Each family and each tribe carefully received its own parcel of land. This was important. The earth belonged to Yahweh, and he gave it to his people justly and fairly because they were equally his children.

The Year of Jubilee. But Yahweh was realistic about all this. He knew that, in the course of time, some would lose their land in debt or sickness. Therefore, he established a law which was truly a revolutionary concept. He proclaimed a Jubilee Year: '' . . . you shall hallow the fiftieth year and proclaim liberation in the land for all its inhabitants. You shall make this your year of jubilee. Every man of you shall return to his patrimony, every man to his family. . . . But if the man cannot afford to buy back the property, it shall remain in the hands of the purchasers till the year of jubilee. It shall then revert to the original owner, and he shall return to his patrimony'' (Leviticus 25:10-28).

The law of private ownership was clearly superseded here by a higher law, namely, that every man had a right to the land of his family. If he lost it and could not buy it back, that land became his again each fiftieth year. Thus, there could be no great fortunes built on the backs of the poor.

Israel, of course, never kept the law very well; and soon the land was filled with injustice. The people cried out to Yahweh against the rich who bound them in a new slavery.

''Happy the man whose helper is the God of Jacob,

   . . . who serves wrongdoers as he has sworn

   and deals out justice to the oppressed.

The LORD feeds the hungry

   and sets the prisoners free. . . .

The LORD loves the righteous

   and watches over the stranger;

the LORD gives heart to the orphan and widow. . .'' (Psalm 146:5-9).

Even the kings whose task it was to mete out justice became a new class of oppressors. By the time of the great prophets, the land — God's own people — was rife with injustice and oppression. The word of the prophets then often became a strong warning against injustice.

The Prophets

The Prophet Isaiah. The great prophet Isaiah spoke of God's scorn for some of Israel's most esteemed institutions — their worship and their fast — because these practices were carried on in the midst of injustice.

"Hear the word of the LORD. . . .

Your countless sacrifices, what are they to me?
    says the LORD.
I am sated with whole-offerings of rams . . .
I have no desire for the blood of bulls. . . .
    The offer of your gifts is useless,
the reek of sacrifice is abhorrent to me. . . .
Though you offer countless prayers,
    I will not listen.
There is blood on your hands;
    wash yourselves and be clean.
Put away the evil of your deeds. . . .
Cease to do evil and learn to do right,
pursue justice and champion the oppressed;
give the orphan his rights, plead the widow's cause"
(Isaiah 1:10-17).

To go again and again to the Temple to offer sacrifice and at the same time to forget God's poor and treat them unjustly was offensive in the eyes of Yahweh.

His words are even sharper in regard to the Israelites' fasting:
"Is it a fast like this that I require,
    a day of mortification such as this,
    that a man should . . . make his bed on sackcloth and
        ashes? . . .

9

Is not this what I require of you as a fast:
to loose the fetters of injustice,
to untie the knots of the yoke,
    to snap every yoke
and set free those who have been crushed?
Is it not sharing your food with the hungry,
taking the homeless poor into your house,
    clothing the naked when you meet them
    and never evading a duty to your kinsfolk?''
(Isaiah 58:5-7)

These texts echo the familiar Old Testament theme: "It is mercy I desire and not sacrifice." To trample on people and call oneself religious was (and is) a contradiction.

Isaiah addressed a situation (much like today's) where an arrogant, upper-class people lived in disregard of the poor. They were church-going people who seemed not to notice the suffering and impoverishment of the many.

Isaiah had few good words for the ruling class.
"The LORD opens the indictment
against the elders of his people and their officers . . . "
Those who should have looked out for the poor
"have ravaged the vineyard,
    and the spoils of the poor are in your houses.
Is it nothing to you that you crush my people
    and grind the faces of the poor?" (Isaiah 3:14-15).
"Shame on you!" he said, "you who add house to house
    and join field to field,
    until not an acre remains,
(for the poor) and you are left to dwell alone in the land" (5:8).

The Prophet Amos. The presence of injustice in the country was especially disturbing to another prophet, Amos. He was a simple man, a shepherd. He saw the heart of Yahweh turned to the poor, and the hearts of many of his countrymen turned against them. The rich,

whose business practices and style of life were the cause of great
mistreatment of the poor, came in for special condemnation.

" . . . For crime after crime of Israel
    I will grant no reprieve,
because they sell the innocent for silver
    and the destitute for a pair of shoes.
They grind the heads of the poor into the earth
    and thrust the humble out of their way . . . "
(Amos 2:6-7).

The rich lived in a splendor which Yahweh promised to destroy.

"I will break down both winter-house and summer-house;
      houses of ivory shall perish,
  and great houses be demolished.
      This is the word of the LORD.
. . . you cows of Bashan who live on the hill of Samaria,
you who oppress the poor and crush the destitute,
  . . . your time is coming
    when men shall carry you away on their shields . . . "
(Amos 3:15-4:1).

The Prophet Jeremiah. Jeremiah adds his note to this chorus of
complaint.

" . . . among my people there are wicked men,
    . . . who set deadly traps to catch men.
Their houses are full of fraud,
as a cage is full of birds.
They grow rich and grand,
    bloated and rancorous;
their thoughts are all of evil,
    and they refuse to do justice,
the claims of the orphan they do not put right
nor do they grant justice to the poor" (Jeremiah 5:26-28).

The Old Testament epoch ends, for all practical purposes, on this
dismal note. The people whose history had begun with their own
liberation from slavery and injustice had themselves become the

11

oppressors of the poor among them. Their kingdoms are destroyed, and their cities too, because they have not heeded the words of the prophets, the words of Yahweh. They are taken into captivity by neighboring nations. Only a remnant will return to carry on a hope for justice that will be embodied in the Messiah-King.

The Messiah, Jesus Christ

The Gospel of Luke. Luke takes up the story from here. He speaks of a Messiah come to bring good news to the poor.

The opening lines of Luke's Gospel show us Jesus taking his place among the poor. His parents are poor in a land still divided between rich and poor. He is born in a stable and laid in a manger. Mary's hymn, known as the Magnificat, serves as a preamble to the theme of Luke's Gospel. It is a Gospel of mercy and of joy. Its focus is on the little ones whose longing for the Lord and his justice will not go unrewarded.

" . . . he has brought down monarchs from their thrones,
    but the humble have been lifted high.
The hungry he has satisfied with good things,
    the rich sent empty away" (Luke 1:52-53).

As Jesus began his public life, he chose a text from Isaiah which clearly defined the scope of his work. The setting was the synagogue in Nazareth. He opened the scroll and found the passage which read:
"The Spirit of the Lord GOD is upon me
because the LORD has anointed me;
he has sent me to bring good news to the humble,
to proclaim liberty to captives
    and release to those in prison;
to proclaim a year of the LORD's favour" (Isaiah 61:1-2).
He is the anointed (the Messiah) sent by the Father to continue the work begun in the Old Testament's central event, the Exodus, and bring it to completion: to save from oppression those whose burdens were too heavy. This was Jesus' self-understanding.

When, a while later, John's disciples came asking who he was so they could tell John, Jesus in a sense repeats this text. " . . . 'Go' he said, 'and tell John what you have seen and heard: how the blind recover their sight, the lame walk, the lepers are made clean, the deaf hear, the dead are raised to life, the poor are hearing the good news' . . . '' (Luke 7:22-23). This is what he was doing. Those that were sick and outcast and poor were receiving the blessing that Yahweh, the God of the poor, had promised. Where kings and institutions had failed, Jesus was bringing hope and freedom.

The Great Discourse. Jesus' great speech in the sixth chapter of Luke begins with the same kind of declaration. There could be no mistaking Jesus' purpose. As the Magnificat had hinted, he would raise up the poor and put down the rich.

" . . . blest are you who are in need; the kingdom of God is yours. . . . blest are you who now go hungry; your hunger shall be satisfied. . . . blest are you who weep now; you shall laugh. . . . But alas for you who are rich; you have had your time of happiness. Alas for you who are well-fed; you shall go hungry. Alas for you who laugh now; you shall mourn and weep'' (Luke 6:20-25).

To understand Jesus without taking into account his own very clear descriptions of himself, his ministry, his values, is to miss the point of Jesus. For many, he is merely an escape from the harshness of this life. These texts, on the other hand, show him involved in real life, in its pain and anguish. The story he tells of the rich man and the beggar, Lazarus, is certainly a lesson on living, not a description of afterlife. It is an example of the blessings and woes just cited. ''There was once a rich man, who dressed in purple and the finest linen, and feasted in great magnificence every day. At his gate, covered with sores, lay a poor man named Lazarus, who would have been glad to satisfy his hunger with the scraps from the rich man's table. Even the dogs used to come and lick his sores. One day the poor man died and was carried away by the angels to be with Abraham. The rich man also died and was buried, and in Hades, where he was in torment, he looked up; and there, far away, was Abraham with Lazarus close behind him. 'Abraham, my father,' he called out, 'take pity on me! Send Lazarus to dip the tip of his finger in water, to cool my tongue, for I am in agony in this fire.' But Abraham said, 'Remember, my child, that all the good things fell to you while you were alive, and all the bad to Lazarus; now he has his consolation here and it is you who are in agony' '' (Luke 16:19-25).

Jesus proposed a style of life that was at odds with the prevailing practice in Israel and the Roman Empire. It continues to cut into the societal norms of our age. It has three components:

1. Sharing Goods. Jesus called for the sharing of surplus goods with the poor. The division of society between rich and poor was repugnant to him as it had been earlier to his Father. His call to ''sell what you have and give it to the poor'' is a way of setting things right again. It is the endless jubilee which he came to proclaim. He called it a ''year of the Lord's favor.'' His disciples understood his message and lived by it. ''We have left our homes and followed you,'' Peter said. Jesus assured him that they would not go unrewarded either in this life or in the next. The early Church also — from the evidence given in Acts of the Apostles — practiced this Messianic counsel: '' . . . they would sell their property and possessions and make a general distribution as the need of each required'' (Acts 2:45). And a little later we read, ''Not a man of them claimed any of his possessions as his own, but everything was held in common. . . . They were all held in high esteem; for they had never a needy person among them . . . '' (Acts 4:32-34).

Jesus was critical of those who store up treasures for themselves on earth (Luke 12:15-21). He said it is more difficult for those who are rich to enter heaven than for a camel to go through the eye of a needle (Luke 18:24-25). All of this he said not because he had it in for the rich but because he and his Father hated the injustice inflicted on the poor. They saw the abundance of the rich as a cause of the suffering of the poor.

The initial reaction of Jesus to the rich young man was one of love. And Jesus praised Zacchaeus when he gave back half of his goods to the poor. Jesus counted Zacchaeus among the saved.

The one time Jesus appears to have been really angry was at the cleansing of the Temple. To know why he was angry we need only listen to what he said: "It is written, 'My house shall be a house of prayer'; but you have made it a den of robbers." What offended him was the fact that the buyers and sellers of the Temple, in collusion with the priests no doubt, were defrauding the poor of their offerings for the Temple sacrifice, and overcharging them. They were robbers of the poor. Amos and Isaiah and Jeremiah had castigated the Israelites for the same kind of sin. Defrauding the poor, taking what little they have, is odious in the eyes of God. The rich who do this merit his severe condemnation.

2. Being Servants. Secondly, Jesus challenged the prevailing norms about the use of power. On one occasion, as his disciples were engaged in a dispute about who was the greatest among them, Jesus said, " . . . In the world, kings lord it over their subjects; and those in authority are called their country's 'Benefactors'. Not so with you: on the contrary, the highest among you must bear himself like the youngest, the chief of you like a servant. For who is greater — the one who sits at table or the servant who waits on him? Surely the one who sits at table. Yet here I am among you like a servant" (Luke 22:25-27).

The understanding of power that Jesus recommends is the exact antithesis of the world's understanding. Rulers lord it over others, the Roman emperors call themselves 'benefactors' — givers of all gifts and holders of all power. Jesus' way is different. He, though evidently the Lord, goes among his followers as the servant. He washes their feet at the Last Supper and says to them when he has finished, "You call me 'Master' and 'Lord', and rightly so, for that is what I am. Then if I, your Lord and Master, have washed your feet, you also ought to wash one another's feet. I have set you an example: you are to do as I have done for you" (John 13:13-15).

As the teaching of Jesus on sharing wealth breaks the spiral of greed that makes for rich and poor, so his teaching on power as service loosens the grip of false political power. Jesus' style of being a servant and calling his disciples into servanthood is a new way of establishing relationships. It contradicts the style embodied in emperors and kings of old and in authoritarian regimes of the present day.

Mark's Gospel is especially insistent on this point. It is a litany that reaches its crescendo of ultimate liberation in the death of the Servant. " . . . If anyone wants to be first, he must make himself last of all and servant of all" (9:35). "Whoever receives one of these children in my name . . . receives me" (9:37). And, " . . . among you, whoever wants to be great must be your servant, and whoever wants to be first must be the willing slave of all. For even the Son of Man did not come to be served but to serve, and to give up his life as a ransom for many" (10:43-45).

3. Standing Up for Justice. A particular application of this teaching of Jesus is his stance toward practical abuses of authority. He was especially critical of the Pharisees who, though they had no direct political authority, still exercised great power within the society. His denunciations of them are unequaled in the Gospels. " . . . You Pharisees! You clean the outside of cup and plate; but inside you there is nothing but greed and wickedness. You fools! Did not he who made the outside make the inside too? But let what is in the cup be given in charity, and all is clean.

"Alas for you Pharisees! You pay tithes of mint and rue and every garden-herb, but have no care for justice and the love of God. It is these you should have practised, without neglecting the others" (Luke 11:39-43).

Moreover, Jesus indicates that his disciples will have to take a stand against the abuses of authority, and will suffer for it. "You will be brought before synagogues and put in prison; you will be haled before kings and governors for your allegiance to me. This will be your opportunity to testify . . . I myself will give you power of utterance and a wisdom which no opponent will be able to resist or refute" (Luke 21:12-15).

Many Christians today, too, in their pursuit of justice for the poor, feel obliged in conscience to take a critical stance toward political authority. This should come as no surprise to a biblical people. When that authority fails to provide justice for the poor, it merits opposition.

Conclusion

This tiny sketch shows that the Bible is not aloof from the problems of justice that plague society, both ancient and modern. Jesus comes as one who calls to conversion. In a world where there is growing tension between rich and poor people and between rich and poor nations, we need to listen to his call.

1. In your personal prayer, reflect on the biblical themes in this chapter. Discuss these themes with a group of friends. Ask yourselves: How do our ideas on justice for the oppressed square with these themes?

2. Discuss the following questions:

What is the law of Jubilee? Are my ideas on private property consistent with the law of Jubilee?

What does Jesus' admonition to sell what I have and give to the poor mean to me in my life situation?

In what way do I serve the poor in my town or city?

What do I do when I learn of public pronouncements and policies that are not consistent with the teaching of Jesus?

Recommended Reading

Richard J. Cassidy, *Jesus, Politics and Society: A Study of Luke's Gospel*. Orbis Books, 1978. Paperback.

Donald B. Kraybill, *The Upside-down Kingdom*. Herald Press, 1978. Paperback.

2
Poverty in the United States

Poverty Among Black People. To speak with pastors whose concerns are inner-city ghettos or rural areas of poverty is to discover a world that many middle-class Americans never see. Father Hilary, Sister Marie, and Reverend Claude all work in the predominantly black area of our city. All three are black and have deliberately chosen their present areas of ministry.

Reverend Claude speaks of the high incidence of unemployment among his people. It is something one can observe just walking through the streets near his church. Unemployment hits especially the young black male. National figures say unemployment among black youth runs to forty-eight percent.

Reverend Claude speaks also of the phenomenon of welfare dependency among his people. Created to help those without jobs and skills, the welfare system has unfortunate side effects. For the sake of survival, fathers often abandon their families. Lives revolve, for generations, around the welfare check.

Sister Marie echoes Reverend Claude's concern about unemployment among black people. She points to one of the biggest businesses in the area and says it does not employ a proportionate number of black people. The same lack of proportion exists in local government. It is far more white than it should be, given the size of the local black population.

Father Hilary agrees with Reverend Claude and Sister Marie about the side effects of high unemployment and low political input. The police system often appears to be the enemy of the black community. Police brutality and harassment are things Father Hilary's parishioners have come to expect. Gang violence is a common outlet for youthful frustration.

All three religious leaders spoke of the sense of despair and the loss of a sense of personal worth among their congregations, especially among unemployed young black males.

Poverty Among Latin People. Pedro and Elena have become friends of ours since they fled El Salvador under death threat and arrived in our city. Joblessness and fear of deportation stalk their days. At the root of this is a problem that many Americans of Latin descent face — that of racism. Referring to a recent crackdown by immigration officials, the chancellor of one western Catholic diocese said, ''I think that in this area the target was quite clearly the Mexican or Mexican-looking person, and obviously that is racist in its conception as well as in its operation . . . Nationally, eighty-seven percent of those caught up in the raids were Hispanic.''

The chancellor of the diocese, himself Hispanic, alluded to another significant area of pastoral concern in the United States — the struggle of Latin peoples. The impoverishment of the Puerto Rican people in New York City and the oppression of farm workers in California are familiar news items, but the poverty of Latins in the United States is far more widespread than that.

The story of Olivia is a case in point. Olivia is a friend and a neighbor of mine. Her family has known much of the pain that Americans of Latin descent suffer. Two of her sons have died. One son was shot in the streets near their home. The other son was shot while in the custody of the county sheriff. Neither case has been fully investigated. Asked if any city official ever came to see her about all this, Olivia responds, ''Just to arrest my kids.'' Only her deep faith in God keeps her going from day to day. So it is with thousands of U.S. citizens of Latin descent.

Poverty Among Working People. Growing poverty among working-class Americans is a third area of concern. In 1975 the Catholic bishops of Appalachia wrote a lament which still applies, and to other parts of the country as well. The bishops' pastoral letter, entitled *This Land Is Home to Me,* includes these poignant words:

> ''In this land of ours,
> jobs are often scarce.
> Too many people are forced

to accept unjust conditions
or else lose their jobs.

Human services for the poor,
and for the almost poor,
are inadequate.
Safety standards
are often too weak,
or ignored.
Workers are injured
unnecessarily.
Legal and medical recourse
for claims against occupational injury
or occupational disease
are often too difficult
or unavailable.
Sometimes
those who should be helping people
in their claims,
seem to stand in the way.
Black Lung
and mine accidents
are the most famous examples,
but not the only ones. . . .

It's strange, for instance . . .
that a country which took such
richness from Appalachia
left so little for the people.
Great fortunes were built
on the exploitation of
Appalachian workers
and Appalachian resources,
yet the land was left
without revenues
to care for its social needs, like

— education
— welfare
— old age
— and illness. . . .

Plain people work hard all their life,
and their parents worked hard before them,
yet they can't make ends meet.
— Food is too expensive.
— Taxes are too high for most.
— (Too low for the rich.)
— Sickness puts people into debt.
— College is out of reach for their children.
— Paychecks keep shrinking.

And it's worse for those who can't work,
especially the elderly.''

What Is Happening Here?

Marginalization. In a land that boasts the highest standard of living in the world there are many people who do not know well-being. For these people poverty and oppression are a daily diet. Why?

In looking to causes of this poverty and injustice, one is first struck by the phenomenon of marginalization; many workers are simply being left on the sidelines in today's economy. Some seem even to be entering the ranks of the permanently unemployable. Among the latter would seem to be the large body of young black men.

A contracting economy is partly to blame here. The number of plant closures and small business bankruptcies certainly contribute to marginalization of workers. But a deeper reason is a need that is not being met for job-retraining in what is a drastically changing economy. Unskilled jobs are at a minimum and old skills that used to provide many jobs — in the steel and auto industries, for example — are simply not needed in what is becoming a heavily computerized world. As a result, many people are left behind as the economy continues to change.

21

Control of the Economy. A second reason for the phenomenon of widespread poverty is that we survive in an economy that maintains the myth of *individualistic capitalism*. In many ways we have moved beyond that. We have large government involvement in the economy — in defense and welfare, for example. Government is also involved in industries that for all practical purposes are public corporations, some with larger Gross National Products than many countries have. These two things have drastically changed what was a free capitalist system. Yet, maintaining the myth of free capitalism has given almost free reign to the large corporations and industries and to the wealthy class who control them. They exercise a control over government and American life which results in the impoverishment of many people. The distance between rich and poor grows. Those at the top of the economy command enormous salaries and stock options out of all proportion to the rest of society. They use tax loopholes to avoid paying their fair share of taxes, often paying less than working-class people pay. Those at the bottom of the ladder barely make ends meet. In the middle is a large population of working people who increasingly feel the squeeze, many of whom are returning to the ranks of the poor.

What is needed is an "economics as if people mattered." This would place people's welfare and job needs above the rights of big business and the maintenance of a wealthy elite. It would cut into the vast discrepancy in salaries. It would put controls of some sort on companies whose unilateral decisions to move or close plants leave whole areas of the country destitute. It would create the kind of economy that makes jobs available to those who want to work, and would help with the retraining needed to fit them into the jobs available in a changing economy.

Powerlessness. Underneath these economic considerations is a political cause of impoverishment of first importance. It is the sense of *powerlessness* in the face of big government and big business that now pervades the atmosphere of the United States. Many citizens simply throw their hands up in despair. "What can I do?" is a common question. There is a widespread sense that the American system of "one person — one vote" is being effectively undermined by powerful interest groups that lobby in favor of the big corporations, the wealthy, and pet projects.

The large drop-off in the number of voters is indicative of this sense of powerlessness. This sense people have is ominous because it is destructive of a democratic society. As a remedy, many are calling for the creation of local structures — neighborhood organizations — where people can begin to make their voices heard again.

Racism. Finally, at the root of much of the present U.S. poverty is *racism* — the cultural phenomenon of seeing other groups or classes of people as undeserving of respect because of their nationality or the color of their skin. Those who are poor in the United States are most often black or brown. The epithets of "lazy poor" are often applied to them. They are the last to be hired and the first to be fired. Often they are seen as a threat to the predominantly white majority. "They will take our jobs." "They pull the neighborhood down."

There is no doubt that we live in a racist society. Blacks made some gains in the 1960s, and Latins are now becoming an effective political voice on their own behalf. But there is still segregation and discrimination in our society on a large scale. Whites live in some sections of our cities, blacks mostly in others. There are Puerto Rican ghettos and Mexican barrios.

Many other causes of poverty among us could be proposed. In this short booklet the four mentioned above will have to suffice: the economics of *marginalization* and *individualism,* political *powerlessness* and the cultural phenomenon of *racism.* We turn our attention now to the Gospel.

From the Perspective of Faith

The Gospel and the Poor. Some people excuse themselves from concern for the poor by citing a text from the New Testament: "You have the poor among you always . . . " (Matthew 26:11). This saying almost seems to approve of poverty. But, in fact, this text is a call to place the Lord first in one's life; it is not an excuse for failing to hear the rest of his word. Just before this passage in Matthew's Gospel, Jesus places the plight of the poor in the context of a judgment scene. He says that Christians who fail to reach out to the poor and oppressed fail to reach out to him. Therefore, they merit condemnation:

" . . . the king will say to those on his right hand, 'You have my Father's blessing; come, enter and possess the kingdom that has been ready for you since the world was made. For when I was hungry, you gave me food; when thirsty, you gave me drink; when I was a stranger you took me into your home, when naked you clothed me; when I was ill you came to my help, when in prison you visited me.' Then the righteous will reply, 'Lord, when was it that we saw you hungry and fed you, or thirsty and gave you drink, a stranger and took you home, or naked and clothed you? When did we see you ill or in prison, and come to visit you?' And the king will answer, 'I tell you this: anything you did for one of my brothers here, however humble, you did for me.' Then he will say to those on his left hand, 'The curse is upon you; go from my sight to the eternal fire that is ready for the devil and his angels. For when I was hungry you gave me nothing to eat, when thirsty nothing to drink; when I was a stranger you gave me no home, when naked you did not clothe me; when I was ill and in prison you did not come to my help.' And they too will reply, 'Lord, when was it that we saw you hungry or thirsty or a stranger or naked or ill or in prison, and did nothing for you?' And he will answer, 'I tell you this: anything you did not do for one of these, however humble, you did not do for me.' And they will go away to eternal punishment, but the righteous will enter eternal life'' (Matthew 25:34-46).

This statement — if listened to — effectively cuts into the individualism, racism, and powerlessness that plague American society. It sets a priority, not on individual and private accumulation of goods, but on the way of sharing and being of service that has long marked Christian history.

The poor may always be with us, but they are a constant invitation to reject the mores of a self-centered society. Because Christ says "the least among you," this text challenges the racism of American society. It is as "the least" that victims of racial prejudice are often perceived. At the bottom of the social ladder and "different" because of their race or language, they easily fall into the category of which Jesus speaks in this judgment passage.

The admonition of Jesus also attacks the sense of powerlessness that grips us. It says: stop wringing your hands and do something. Go be among the poor. Get out of your comfortable place and find them in their hunger and in their prisons, and do something for them.

This simple instruction presupposes something very important. It presupposes that we enter the world of the poor from which we are often isolated. The poor live — for the most part — in places where middle-class America does not live. We may pass through their ghettos on the way to the city, but we never really enter their world.

To make an option for the poor is to follow the Christ who came to bring them Good News. He counseled his disciples to imitate his own option for the poor: " . . . sell your possessions, and give to the poor . . . and come follow me." Care and concern for the poor is clearly a Christian imperative. The Gospel clearly calls us to take our place among the poor.

Church Teaching and the Poor. In reflecting on the Gospel, the popes and bishops have focused a dimension that merits serious consideration. There are *structures of poverty* that need our attention. It is not enough to help individuals in need without paying attention to the economic, political, and cultural causes of continuing poverty.

A black pastor told me a story that rises from the black tradition in America. The story visualizes what is meant by structural causes. There were townspeople, the story goes, who were living by the side of a great river. Each morning they would find bodies floating down the river. As good Christian people they would go out, get the bodies, and care for them. Those that were dead they would bury; those that were still alive they would nurse back to health. This went on for many years. But in all that time the townspeople never went upstream

25

to find out what caused the bodies to come floating down the river in the first place.

If we are really concerned for the poor, we will go upstream and get at those causes that are structural in nature.

John Paul II writes: "So widespread is the phenomenon (of poverty) that it brings into question the financial, monetary, production and commercial mechanisms that, resting on various political pressures, support the world economy. These are proving incapable either of remedying the unjust social situations inherited from the past or of dealing with the urgent challenges and ethical demands of the present . . . These structures unceasingly make the areas of misery spread, accompanied by anguish, frustration, and bitterness" (*Redemptor Hominis*, 16).

There are, the Pope says, structures in society that produce poverty, at least as a side effect. One such structure is an economic system based on greed. "Indeed," writes John Paul, "everyone is familiar with the picture of the consumer civilization, which consists in a certain surplus of goods necessary for people and for entire societies — and we are dealing precisely with the rich, highly developed societies — while the remaining societies — at least broad sectors of them — are suffering from hunger, with many people dying each day of starvation and malnutrition" (*Redemptor Hominis*, 16).

An economic system that promotes such flagrant consumption while many people go hungry is, in the Pope's view, wrong and should be corrected. The staggering differences between rich and poor people, between rich and poor nations, need drastic correction at the level of the structures which cause these disparities.

Another serious cause of poverty, in Pope John Paul's view, is the enormous outlay of money for military arms. This takes food out of the mouths of the poor. "We all know well," he states, "that the areas of misery and hunger on our globe could have been made fertile in a short time, if the gigantic investments for armaments at the service of war and destruction had been changed into investment for food at the service of life" (*Redemptor Hominis*, 16).

The need of nations to arm themselves in terms of billions of dollars depends on the need to secure access to the world's increasingly limited goods. In place of this, a strengthened world government could do much to resolve conflicts and assure each nation an ample supply of goods for its survival. The concept of nationalism is becoming outworn in a global village. The time is coming for stronger global cooperation.

What Can We Do?

It is often difficult to know where to begin when faced with huge problems, and the plight of the poor among us is certainly a huge problem. Here are some simple suggestions that may help you get started.

1. Make an option for the poor in the way you live. Begin to hear the Lord's word about selling what you have and giving it to the poor — and do just that. Change from being a person who accumulates things to one who begins to do with less. Talk with your family about this. Examine your home and your life-style for things that might be given or given up for those who have less.

2. Make an option for the poor by beginning to know who the poor are in your area. Find out where they live. Begin to know them personally. Go among them and be present to them. Find out their needs. Let their joys and their hopes, their griefs and their anxieties become yours. Find some like-minded people in your neighborhood to go with you and, together, begin to make a difference in the lives of the poor.

3. Support legislators who act in favor of the poor. Quiz local leaders and national representatives on these matters of poverty. Support those with new, creative ideas that counteract structures in society which impoverish people.

4. Form a group to discuss this chapter. Share your thoughts and any experience of poverty you have had in your life.

Points for Discussion

1. Pages 18-21 describe aspects of poverty in the United States: unemployment, the struggle of Latin peoples, and poverty among

working-class people. Discuss these realities, giving examples from personal experience or from the media.

2. If you were to write a pastoral letter along the lines of *This Land Is Home to Me* (pages 19-21), what conditions in your own region would you focus on?

3. Pages 21-23 list four causes of poverty in the United States. Discuss these causes and give examples from personal experience or from the media.

4. Discuss Pope John Paul II's statement in paragraph 16 of *Redemptor Hominis* (page 26 of this chapter). In discussing, recall: $17 billion *a year* could feed, clothe, house, educate, and provide medical care for *every human being on earth* — $17 billion are spent on military arms *every two weeks*.

Recommended Reading

Arthur Simon, *Bread for the World*. Paulist Press and Wm. B. Eerdmans Publishing Co., 1975. Paperback.

To Do the Work of Justice. A Plan of Action for the Catholic Community in the United States. Office of Publishing Services, United States Catholic Conference. Catalog No. B-132. $1.25.

Isidro Lucas, *The Browning of America: The Hispanic Revolution in the American Church*. Twenty-Third Publications, 1981. Paperback.

Robert Hutchinson, *What One Christian Can Do About Hunger in America*. Twenty-Third Publications, 1981. Paperback.

Tom Blackburn, *Christian Business Ethics: Doing Good While Doing Well*. Twenty-Third Publications, 1981. Paperback.

3
Latin America: The Cry for Justice

My impressions of Latin America begin with José Juan. I met and heard of many José Juans several years ago while staying with missionaries in the Dominican Republic. His story is an example of life in the Americas to the south of us. I quote here from Laurence Simon's "Plantation Politics in the Dominican Republic," *New World Outlook,* vol. 34, no. 3, November 1973, pages 1-3.

José Juan

"The Hotel La Romana stands like a mirage against a sea of cane fields. There is a high fence around the hotel grounds but armed guards casually wave the white American past the gate.

"Many of the guests arrive in their private jets on a small landing strip that bisects the Pete Dye-designed golf course. Others dock their yachts at the private marina on the Caribbean. . . .

"The hotel, sugar mill, and 275,000 acres of surrounding land are owned by Gulf & Western Americas Corporation, part of Gulf & Western Industries Inc., with assets in 1972 of almost \$2.3 billion.

"José Juan lives in a battey, or small congregation of dwellings, near the town of El Siebo. He has never dined at the grand hotel, swum at their private beach nor for that matter has he ever seen it. Sr. Juan lives alone in a shack unfit for human habitation. . . . José Juan is a cane cutter and an employee of Gulf & Western Americas Corporation. And José Juan is dying. . . .

"He came to work for 'the company' as a cane cutter in 1914. One can see that his body was once strong and firm. But the years . . . have taken their toll. He is weak and in pain. He is frightened he will die in his lonely shack. Without strength he does not work and cannot earn his meager wages. He has nothing to eat but the scraps his neighbors, who are as poor as he, bring to him in pity. . . . José Juan usually goes hungry.

"Having heard about a company hospital he begs his visitors to help him gain admittance. But the local priest informs him that the company says it is only for employees and José Juan has not worked in over a year.

"He insists he is due a pension. The priest explains that the company grants a $6 per month pension for an employee who has worked 48 years or more. But again the management says that records were poorly kept so many years ago, and José Juan must be patient while they investigate.

"But it is difficult to ask a dying man for patience.

"Charles G. Bluhdorn lives in a duplex penthouse on the fashionable East Side of Manhattan. He is also an employee of Gulf & Western Industries. As Chairman of the Board he earned $252,600 for the fiscal year ending July 31, 1972. This sum does not reflect such benefits as stock options and savings plans (which would bring his yearly income to approximately $600,000). When Mr. Bluhdorn retires, it is estimated he will receive $74,829 per annum in pension benefits. He will not go hungry. . . . "

Another impression of Latin America begins with Pio. He was a young Guatemalan catechist, a leader in the local Christian community. As things began to heat up between the Church and the Guatemalan military, Pio told his friends, "I am willing to die." Soon after, his body was found along a country road. Stuffed into his lifeless hand was a hit list, on which was the name of Edgar Buch.

Edgar Buch

Edgar Buch (an alias used for his protection) is a Mayan Indian and a Catholic priest. Sixty-five percent of the Guatemalan population is Mayan. Yet this majority experiences incredible prejudice and persecution from the Ladino (Spanish-speaking non-Indian) minority which holds power in the country. Edgar himself experienced this cruelty as an eleven-year-old when he was stripped and ridiculed by Ladino classmates in the town square, and when exploited by owners while working with his father in the west of Guatemala. The discrimination followed him into the seminary where an archbishop said, "How can you bring Indians into the seminary?" Ladinos tried to kill Edgar before his ordination for fear that he, an educated Mayan, would awaken his people to the terrible injustice in which they lived. When his name was found on the death list he was a parish priest active in the Charismatic renewal and in the formation of catechists. Pio was one of those catechists.

According to Father Buch, an average of 300 Mayans are murdered each day. Since the U.S.-backed military take-over in 1954, there have been about 80,000 such murders in Guatemala. The Mayans have been pushed back over the years to the altiplano area bordering Mexico. Ladinos own the rich western farmland. The U.S.-owned United Fruit Company is in the east. Until recently the altiplano was considered useless. Now newly discovered zinc, oil, nickel, and uranium are making this one of the most coveted parts of the country, and the Indians' lands are being ruthlessly taken over by the military, with ex-president General Lucas Garcia in the forefront of this operation.

Such is the life Father Buch and his people have come to know. In a land that was once theirs they are now the enemy of those who hold power, hunted and killed, driven from the little land left to them. In one of the richest countries of Central America, Father Buch sees nothing ahead but misery for his people. The polarization in his country is extreme: the haves against the have-nots; the military against the guerilla; the government against the Church; U.S. businesses protecting their interests. All of this promises many more years of bloodshed.

For Edgar Buch, however, the story is interrupted for awhile. When the death list with his name on it was found, his bishop asked Father Buch to leave Guatemala. Traveling by night and hiding with relatives, he made his way to the airport. He was unable to contact his mother for fear of being caught by the military. With a heavy heart, he was about to board the plane when he looked around one last time and saw his mother standing there. A brother with whom Edgar had stayed the night before had brought her to the airport. Over the objections of the guard, Edgar ran back to embrace his mother in a teary farewell. He has not heard from his family since.

The Cause of Injustice

The stories of Edgar Buch and José Juan are the stories of much of
Latin America. What is happening is that a vast population of poor
people is awakening to the life of oppression in which they have been
held. The countries of Latin America differ from one another more
than our stereotypes often suggest. But there are certain elements
common to their story.

1. The Wealthy Few. The first of these common elements is: *too
much of the land and other means of production are owned by too few
people*. There is a vast difference separating the owner class and the
poor in Latin America. In some places there is a large middle class,
but in most places there is not. Often a few families own most of the
land and business and live in incredible wealth.

At the other end of the economic ladder is a huge population of
very poor people who have little or nothing. For example, in Nicaragua, before the 1979 revolution, the Somoza family owned almost
everything. In El Salvador, there are fourteen families that form a
tight oligarchy. These families keep most of the 4.5 million remaining people impoverished. Father Buch says that ninety percent of the
farm land in Guatemala is owned by two percent of the population.
This situation repeats itself again and again.

2. Miliary Regimes. Tied to this first element is a second that also
holds true for much of Central and South America: *Latin American
countries are marked by the presence of powerful military establish-
ments that side with the wealthy class and often control the government*. This is true in the hot spots that have been in the news of late —
El Salvador, Guatemala, and Argentina. It is true in many other areas
as well. The military sees itself as the savior of the status quo, of law
and order, against the rising tide of unrest among the poor. Often the
regular army, trained by U.S. military personnel, is assisted by
private armies that are paid for — as in El Salvador — by the ruling
class. Over the last few years, this military right-wing presence has
been responsible for thousands of murders in El Salvador and thou-

sands more in Guatemala. In Nicaragua, Somoza's military strafed whole barrios (poor neighborhoods) in Managua, killing thousands more. Brazil's military government has been responsible for brutal torture and murder of opposition leaders, among them priests and bishops.

It is impossible to total the score of violent repression waged against the poor and those who speak for them by Latin American military regimes. Amnesty International, the London-based watchdog on human rights, comes closest to knowing the full record. Amnesty International gives most regimes in Latin America high marks for violence.

Our press, on the other hand, puts great emphasis on the presence of guerilla forces, but these are often poorly armed and poorly organized in comparison to the U.S.-armed-and-trained government military operations in these countries. The power lies with the military and the wealthy elites, and their way is one of violence.

3. Multinational Corporations. A third characteristic that is common to the Latin American scene is the *presence of foreign-owned multinational companies that dominate the economies of these poorer nations*. These companies sometimes bring the illusion of development, but their overall policies do the opposite. Latin American bishops have had this to say about the multinationals in their now famous Medellin Documents:

"Some foreign companies working in our country (also some national firms) often evade the established tax system by subterfuge. We are also aware that at times they send their profits and dividends abroad, without contributing adequate reinvestments to the progressive development of our countries" (Medellin Documents: Peace, 9).

Profits in large amounts are taken out of the country, not left where they rightfully belong. Those who benefit most within the country are the wealthy landowning class, not the poor who are often driven from their lands to make room for plantations of exportable products.

Some countries — like the Dominican Republic — used to be almost self-sufficient in foods for their own use. Now they must import food at prices the poor can ill afford. Many of the newer multinational companies come to find cheap labor — like José Juan — and merely contribute to the existing economic oppression of the poor.

4. Unfair Trade. A fourth element contributing to the unjust condition of the Latin American poor is that *the system of trade between rich and poor nations is itself often unfair.* The rich countries charge much for manufactured products and pay little for the raw materials found in the poorer countries. Foreign aid is often a form of economic slavery, giving rise to burdensome debts which the poorer nations find it impossible to pay. Recent popes have recognized the injustices worked against the so-called developing countries of the south. Pope Paul VI's remarks are particularly thought-provoking: " . . . nations whose industrialization is limited are faced with serious difficulties when they have to rely on their exports to balance their economy and to carry out their plan for development. The poor nations remain ever poor while the rich ones become still richer . . . the rule of free trade, taken by itself, is no longer able to govern international relations . . . industrially developed countries see in it a law of justice. But the situation is no longer the same when economic conditions differ too widely from country to country: prices which are "freely" set in the market can produce unfair results. One must recognize that it is the fundamental principle of liberalism" — the Pope's word for capitalism — "as the rule for commercial exchange, which is questioned here" (*Populorum Progressio,* 57 and 58).

For a nation whose political and business leaders so often invoke the maxims of free trade and individualistic capitalism, these statements of Paul VI give food for serious thought.

The Awakening

For long years the Latin American poor have labored in the hopelessness of their plight. In recent years, however, they have begun to awaken to its injustice. Many things have brought about this awakening — not least of which has been the invasion from the United States of movies and advertising. These media show people the stark contrast between their poverty and the wealth of the more fortunate.

An important factor, too, has been the Catholic Church. The traditional role of the Church in Latin America has been to side with the wealthy class and the status quo. Often the hierarchy came from the upper classes and their allegiance clearly remained there.

But things have changed. The most dramatic change came at the conference of bishops from all over Latin America held in Medellin, Colombia, in 1968. The documents that resulted from the Medellin (pronounced Meh-deh-YEEN) conference placed the Church squarely on the side of the poor. Their struggle for justice was the struggle of the Church. "The misery that besets large masses of human beings in all of our countries . . . expresses itself as injustice which cries to the heavens." "The Latin American Church has a message for all men on this continent who 'hunger and thirst after justice.' The very God who creates men in his image and likeness, creates the 'earth and all that is in it' for the use of all men and all nations, in such a way that created goods can reach all in a more just manner . . . It is the same God who, in the fullness of time, sends his Son in the flesh, so that He might come to liberate all men from the slavery to which sin has subjected them: hunger, misery, oppression and ignorance, in a word, that injustice and hatred which have their origin in human selfishness" (Medellin Documents: Justice, 2 and 3).

The bishops, after reviewing the situation of their countries, took a pastoral stance that was an about-face for them and their churches. They moved from the status quo into the revolutionary spirit that was beginning to mark Latin America. Up to that time — 1968 — they had been close to the rich elites who controlled the countries and oppressed the poor. Now they made an option for the poor. "The Church — the People of God — will lend its support to the down-trodden of every social class so that they might come to know their rights and how to make use of them'' (Medellin Documents: Justice, 20).

The task of *conscientizacion* would be the task of the Church. This means making the poor aware of their situation and of their rights. It would be a policy that often put the Church in direct face-to-face opposition to the wealthy elite and the military regimes which protected them.

An about-face of this nature does not happen all at once, and many prelates still side with the wealthy. For the Church in Latin America this new policy would initiate an era of persecution unlike anything the Church has known since the earliest years of communism in eastern Europe. Ironically, the Latin American bishops would come to be called ''Communist.''

In the decade following Medellin, catechists, lay leaders of Christian communities, priests and Sisters and bishops would be killed by those whose interests were threatened by the poor being made aware of injustice. The epithet of communism would follow Church people everywhere. In the United States press, and in private conversation, we find the Latin American Church accused of being ''Communist'' — when all they have decided to do is to hear the ''cries of the poor.''

This judgment was understandable, even if blatantly wrong. The life-and-death struggle of Latin America to emerge from poverty and from U.S. domination means a fundamental change for American business and the U.S. way of life. Not many in North America welcome this change. Many bitterly oppose it, preferring to subjugate a continent of poor people for selfish gain. Without cheap labor markets and the unlimited raw materials that poorer countries in Latin America provide, our economic machine must drastically change. Already the effects are being felt in higher prices for the raw materials we devour in North America. These effects will go on being felt as the poor go on struggling to shake off oppression. We in North America have lived too long on the backs of the poor to the south of us. José Juan's and Edgar Buch's people are struggling to be free — and part of the freedom they seek is liberation from us.

Liberation Theology

The cry of the poor is one that reaches to the heavens. In ancient Egypt the cries of the Israelites in slavery invoked the great liberation movement of the Old Testament — the deliverance of Yahweh's people from slavery. Today's attempt to build an economic system based on justice for the poor has roots in the Gospel of Jesus as well. Solidarity with the poor is, for example, an essential element of Luke's understanding of Good News. In Luke, Mary describes what God is doing in history:

" . . . the deeds his own right arm has done
    discloses his might:
the arrogant of heart and mind he has put to rout,
he has brought down monarchs from their thrones,
    but the humble have been lifted high.
The hungry he has satisfied with good things,
    the rich sent empty away" (Luke 1:51-53; see also Luke
        4:18 and 7:18-23).

Today in Latin America a new voice, called liberation theology, is heard in the land. It is a theology that finds its roots in the Word of God, taking the poor and their cry as its starting point. It is a voice which listens clearly to the prophets who condemn injustice, sees the liberating dimension of the Scriptures, and discovers a Jesus for whom the poor are the object of special compassion.

Liberation theology calls for a fundamental conversion in the life of the Church, a conversion to the spirit of Jesus. It is clear that Jesus wanted justice and freedom from oppression for the poor and the "little ones" of the kingdom. Liberation theology is a cogent reminder of these truths.

Pope John Paul II has seconded these efforts. When he visited Mexico in 1979, the poverty of the Oaxaca and Chiapas Indians deeply moved the Pope. In a speech he was giving, he departed from his prepared text and said, "With (Pope Paul VI) I would like to reiterate — with an even stronger emphasis in my voice, if that were possible — that the present pope wishes to be (quoting Paul VI) 'in solidarity with your cause, which is the cause of humble people, the poor people.' I wish to reiterate that the pope is with the masses of people who are 'almost always left behind in an ignoble standard of living and sometimes harshly treated and exploited' . . . I adopt the view of my predecessors, John XXIII and Paul VI, and of Vatican II. Seeing a situation that remains alarming, that is seldom better and sometimes worse, the pope chooses to be your voice, the voice of those who cannot speak and who have been silenced. He wishes to be the conscience of consciences; an invitation to action, to make up for lost time, which has frequently been a time of prolonged sufferings and unsatisfied hopes.''

Time for Action

What can we do? In the face of these monumental injustices we feel powerless. Yet there are things we can do.

1. The U.S. Catholic bishops have set good leadership in the area of the Latin American crisis. Listen to them. Read what they have to say.

2. Reject the notion (prevalent in our press and among some U.S. citizens) that there are Communists hiding behind every tree. There may indeed be Communists involved in the struggle in Latin America. But that struggle is rooted in the legitimate right of its people, the vast majority of its people, to seek justice.

3. Challenge our government when it sends military and economic aid to repressive governments in Latin America. The U.S. government often sends such aid to protect American multinational corporations at the expense of the Latin poor. Christians of North America can make their voices heard in defense of our brothers and sisters who suffer at the hands of large business corporations. You can make a difference by writing or calling officials in Washington, protesting aid to repressive regimes. (Washington addresses are as follows. To contact the President, write or call: The White House, 1600 Pennsylvania Avenue, Washington, D.C. 20500; phone 202/456-1414. To contact members of the House and Senate, write or call: House of Representatives, Washington, D.C. 20515; phone

202/224-3121 — U.S. Senate, Washington, D.C. 20510; phone 202/224-3121.)

4. Acknowledge the rights of refugees to find safety in this country — not just refugees from Communist regimes, but those from oppressive right-wing regimes in Latin America as well.

5. Pray. Pray that those who hunger and thirst for justice may be satisfied (see Matthew 5:6).

Points for Discussion

1. The sections on José Juan and Edgar Buch (pages 29-31) present a picture and facts that most North Americans are not very familiar with. How much do your local newspaper and TV news programs help you to get a true picture of what is happening in Latin America?
2. Pages 32-34 outline four causes of the injustice that pervades Latin America. Take each cause one by one and discuss: How aware were we of this situation before we read these pages?
3. The section "The Awakening" on pages 34-36 tells of the "option for the poor" that began with the Medellin conference of 1968. To what extent does this about-face by the Latin American Church help you to understand the turmoil and bloodshed taking place?
4. After reading pages 37-38, what do you think of Liberation Theology?

Recommended Reading

Jack Nelson, *Hunger for Justice*. Orbis Books, 1980. Paperback.

Penny Lernoux, *Cry of the People: The Struggle for Human Rights in Latin America — the Catholic Church in Conflict with U.S. Policy.* Penguin, 1982. Paperback.

Statement of the United States Catholic Conference on Central America. (English and Spanish texts combined.) Office of Publishing Services, United States Catholic Conference. Catalog No. 831. $1.25.

4
The Challenge of Grassroots Christian Communities

The townspeople hurried along the dusty road just as dark began to fall. They chatted excitedly as they walked. Turning a corner, they met friends going in the same direction. They embraced affectionately in the evening light and started again toward their destination.

Just ahead, light spilled from the doorway of a nondescript tin-roofed building next to the old village church. Already the noise of many voices filled the streets outside the building. The newcomers entered and began the round of greeting and embracing.

Thirty or forty people were in the room. Most were standing. Some were already seated on wooden benches that lined the walls or on old school desks in the center of the room. Soon a man called the meeting to order. A guitarist somewhere in the corner plunked out the chords to a song, and they all began to sing.

José, the leader, said a prayer, asking the Lord to bless this meeting of the community. He spoke briefly, asking them to share their concerns. One by one, men and women began to speak. The others listened respectfully as each addressed the group. Some were impassioned, some matter-of-fact, but all spoke at least a word or two. There was sickness in some families, blessings had come to others. A son had left for the city. An old man had died. But mostly talk was about the need for a new bridge. The old bridge, connecting some of the farms with the village, had been washed away in the spring rains. A neighboring community had protested in front of the regional commandant's office, but nothing had been done. The bridge was important if the farmers, members of the community, were to bring their food to the village market. Something must be done.

Others spoke of the watch at the jail. That was going well. The two

French missionary priests — imprisoned for speaking out against a local government scandal — had not been moved. As long as people kept vigil around the clock at the prison, the officials would not dare move the priests. If the officials did move them, the townspeople knew they would never hear of the priests again. So many hundreds of people disappeared while under detention. Their bodies were sometimes found, but most often they were not. They just disappeared. The vigil at the jail was keeping the officials honest and the missionaries alive.

Then someone spoke again of the bridge. Why not build it ourselves? The protests weren't working. There was a mill nearby — they could get the beams there, perhaps on a time payment. They would be expensive. A builder in the town had an old pile driver in his yard. Perhaps they could borrow it. He didn't use it much anymore. Soon they were in agreement. Several people volunteered to begin the work of getting the timbers and the pile driver.

The leader broke in. It was getting late — nearly two hours had gone by. It was time to turn to the Scripture. Several people picked up Bibles and opened them. One reader read a passage about a donkey that fell into the well on the Sabbath. The people listened. Someone from a bench by the wall commented, "Surely the Lord would want us to help our brothers and sisters who farm on the other side of the river. I think he will bless our efforts to build a bridge."

A woman read a passage from a Psalm. It was about the Lord hearing the cries of the poor and bringing justice. Her husband said, "The Lord is hearing us tonight, and people like us all over Brazil." Others read and spoke. All listened carefully and nodded agreement.

When the reading was over, the leader motioned to the guitarist who began another song. The leader opened a little metal container on the table in front of him as they sang. When they finished singing, the leader said a prayer to Jesus, their Brother. Then the leader distributed communion, consecrated a few days ago by a priest who had visited the village. The guitarist started another song. Everyone was quiet. Someone prayed for the sick and for the priests in jails. The final hymn was a stirring one. They stood while they sang it. The

41

song spoke of Jesus sending them forth and going with them, of their hope and their victory.

All over Latin America grassroots Christian communities are manifesting a life that is truly impressive. There are eighty thousand or more in Brazil alone, thousands of others in El Salvador and Chile and Peru and Guatemala. They are the hope of the Church there, of the people themselves. They are a new spring.

But the phenomenon is not limited to Latin America, even though it is most advanced there. In a place as geographically and culturally distant as Krakow, Poland, Cardinal Wojttyla — now Pope John Paul II — started hundreds of small grassroots communities. These communities in various parts of the world are bringing hope and new life to the Church, and becoming a force to be reckoned with by oppressive governments on both the right and the left.

The elements of these grassroots communities are simple: ordinary people, their concerns, their love for one another, the Bible read and shared, working together to bring about a difference in their lives. They are much like the little communities of early Christians that Luke describes in Acts of the Apostles: places of simple faith, sharing of simple lives. In Brazil and elsewhere they have become — in all their simplicity — a threat to those who oppress the poor.

The Challenge of Grassroots Christian Communities

Some people see these small Church communities, springing up in Latin America and all over the world, as a challenge to the Church at large. Those within the Church who see them as a threat fail to understand how they embody much of what the Second Vatican Council and recent popes have challenged the Church to become. I will speak of this challenge under five headings.

1. They are communities of believers. The grassroots Christian communities are places of deeply personalized and renewed faith. For their members, God is their own loving Father, who concerns himself with their lives and their history. He is a God who has given the earth equally to all, the poor as well as the rich. He is a Father to all people; sinful injustice is the cause of inequality. It is not his design.

In Jesus they have come to know a liberator. Jesus came to bring good news to the poor. He epitomizes the liberating work of the Bible. He is on the side of the little ones in their struggle for justice. When they strive to free themselves from economic oppression and political repression, he is a Brother struggling with them. When they suffer and die to set others free, it is his Passion and death that they relive. The liberation that comes is evidence of his Resurrection.

They are a people God loves, called to love one another by standing against the forces who injure their brothers and sisters. Each member of the community has gifts and talents, a voice and time, to use for the liberation of all.

In seeing themselves in this way, they challenge the institutional side of the Church which has at times adopted a stance that mirrors the world more than Christ. This is a world of haves and have-nots, where a few have most of the wealth and means of production; where the many receive merely leftovers, what trickles down to them.

In a similar way, many people once saw the Church as "belonging" to the hierarchy and the clergy, while the people were the "recipients" of grace and the sacraments. The grassroots communities are challenging the Church to remember that all are brothers and sisters; that each person is gifted and has something to offer for the liberation and salvation of others.

2. They are communities of the poor and despoiled. It is the "little ones" who make up these communities: peasants in Latin America; working people in Poland. Those who have been dispossessed of land and labor — those who know oppression, bitter toil, and hunger each day of their lives — have banded together to support each other.

In banding together, they challenge a Church which in Latin America has often allied itself with the rich and the powerful. In the past, many of the clergy came from the families of the wealthy and, at least indirectly, defended the government in its systematic oppression of the poorer classes. To the poor the clergy said, "You will have your reward in heaven." To the rich it said, "Your duty is to be generous." Seldom did the injustice of the societal structures themselves — that a few own almost everything — come up for scrutiny. It was a given fact, and the Church must help people to live with the facts — as if God had sent Moses to Egypt to counsel the Israelite slaves to be patient! The grassroots Church communities challenge this kind of thinking.

3. The grassroots communities have made an option for the poor. They themselves are the poor. But even more, they have opted to be on the side of the poor. In this they challenge a Church which has, at times, been too content with the world's standard of upward mobility and consumerism. Pope John Paul II views consumerism as one of the great evils affecting the Western World. It is the sickness of wanting more and more material things. It is the selfishness of leaving the pack to move ahead for one's own gain, of seeing one's worth measured in terms of having more. The grassroots communities say no to this individualism. They concern themselves with the community, with standing up and moving forward together. A gain for all is a gain for each one.

4. They follow Jesus and listen to his Word. Grassroots communities see themselves as disciples, a word which Pope John Paul II uses to describe the Church. When all is said and done, after all the fine biblical images of the Church have been explained and pondered over, who are we but people who follow Jesus and try to make his Word first in our lives? The grassroots communities are Bible-based. The Bible is part of their lives. It reveals the good news of liberation and is a constant source of direction in their meetings.

Being Bible-based, grassroots communities challenge a Church which can put law and custom above the Word of God. A recent book, *The Gospel of Solentiname*, shows how the Word of God takes root in one Nicaraguan village and becomes the textbook for the people's life together. The community gathers around the Word. They read it and study it. They talk about it and find their world in its pages. Laws can easily stifle. Apathy and death creep into Christian life — on Sunday morning and elsewhere — when the Word is not alive among the people. The grassroots Christian communities challenge the Church to find again the Jesus whose Word cuts into life and brings hope.

5. Grassroots communities take a critical stance. They engage in a style of life that enables them both to see things as they are and to take action when needed. Their own life experience is their starting point. Their meetings begin with a sharing of personal experiences, an account of what is happening in their lives, and what they have observed. In doing this, they see the injustice and oppression that fill their days and affect their families and friends. As they listen to each other, they begin to pinpoint the structures of oppression: an economic system which puts too much in too few hands; a government which represses dissent, as in Brazil and Poland and many other places. They see in their Scripture a God who finds such situations abominable, a Jesus who came to set people free. This is the first thing they see.

These communities, however, do not simply reflect on what is happening and why. They act. They decide what they can do to change situations of oppression and poverty. The last part of their meetings are like planning sessions for a community project. Then they leave and get to work. They protest government abuses or build a bridge or guard a prison. And, in acting together, they begin to see a second thing: they have power. Working together they have the capacity to change things. When they return to their next community meeting, they find that their new experience of acting together has been empowering. Things have changed. They are no longer pawns in someone else's game.

This last aspect of the grassroots communities challenges the Church in two ways. It challenges the powerlessness that is often a part of modern life in the face of big governments, big economic systems, big multinational companies, and long-established customs. People, even the poor, can make a difference. These communities of faith prove this over and over both in their martyrdom and in their joy. Gustavo Gutierrez, a Peruvian theologian, says: "In Nicaragua, for example, one of the most impressive things is the joy of a people who are fighting unto death to be masters of their country and to construct a just society. This joy is also evident in their celebration of the faith. It is the subversive joy of the people, who know that they will rejoice tomorrow, even though they may be weeping today. Their joy subverts a world of oppression. It upsets those exercising domination, denounces the fear of the hesitant, and reveals the love of the God of hope."

The grassroots communities challenge the Church in still another way. They dare it to give up its ties to what is sometimes called "patriotic religion." This is the religious viewpoint that identifies "God and my country." It is implicit in the belief of many that "God is on our side," that our government (whichever one it is) is always in the right, that dissent and protest against an established government is always (or nearly always) wrong. This kind of religion is a perversion that has put country in the place of God and desperately tries to hold on to the status quo. It is often the religion of those who seek to protect their own privileged place in society.

These grassroots communities, then, present an enormous challenge to established structures and to the Church itself. Will it become the Church of the poor? Will it keep faith in the God who is the Father of all and faith in Jesus who liberated the poor? Will it take his Word as seriously as he meant it to be taken? Will it stand up against the oppression and repression it meets in society? Will it accept the challenge to follow Christ?

Acts of the Apostles

In presenting this huge challenge, the grassroots Christian communities of the world remain, in themselves, small and seemingly inconsequential. As such, they are very much like the early communities of believers which we mentioned before. In Acts of the Apostles, Saint Luke described them this way:

"They met constantly to hear the apostles teach, and to share the common life, to break bread, and to pray. A sense of awe was everywhere, and many marvels and signs were brought about through the apostles. All whose faith had drawn them together held everything in common: they would sell their property and possessions and make a general distribution as the need of each required. With one mind they kept up their daily attendance at the temple, and, breaking bread in private houses, shared their meals with unaffected joy, as they praised God and enjoyed the favour of the whole people. And day by day the Lord added to their number those whom he was saving" (Acts 2:42-47).

A little later in Acts, Luke says:

"The whole body of believers was united in heart and soul. Not a man of them claimed any of his possessions as his own, but everything was held in common, while the apostles bore witness with great power to the resurrection of the Lord Jesus. They were all held in high esteem; for they had never a needy person among them, because all who had property in land or houses sold it, brought the proceeds of the sale, and laid the money at the feet of the apostles; it was then distributed to any who stood in need" (Acts 4:32-35).

These two passages are quoted at length in order to let the text show how similar these communities are to the ones developing today. There was (and is) a real sense of shared life, of shared prayer, of the power of the Word among them. There was (and is) a sense that they were all in this together, and they needed to help one another. There was (and is) a sense that each person is someone to be cherished and respected, that each has something to offer.

The sharing of material goods is particularly notable in both passages from Acts of the Apostles. The love those early Christians had for one another (and the love in grassroots communities) was not (and is not) an ethereal love. What bound them together was real. It made demands upon each one. The New Testament Letter of Saint James says it is not enough to see "a brother or sister in rags with not enough food for the day'' and just to say to him ''Good luck!'' The early communities knew that real Christian love demands an option for the poor. Today's communities are learning that. They are the poor, conscious of the poor among them, and sharing what they have in goods and energy, in faith and love.

What Can We Do?

It would be easy to say, ''Go out and start a grassroots community in your neighborhood or parish.'' But doing it is not easy. No community grows overnight or without a lot of blood, sweat, and tears. But here are some things you might try:

1. Pass this booklet on to some others you think might be interested and then see how they react. If their reaction is favorable, start meeting and follow this simple plan:

    a. Share your experiences of need and your feelings of powerlessness.

    b. Try to figure out together what is the cause of these situations. If several of you are experiencing the same thing, perhaps there are injustices built into your world which need correcting.

    c. Open your Bibles to find passages that have some bearing on what you are experiencing. Or take the readings from the Mass for that day and see if they do not speak to your experience.

    d. Plan some action together to confront the injustices you see around you. Meet with the persons responsible, and protest the injustice. Try to change the structure, or at least make its injustice known.

2. Take this booklet to your pastor and see if you can get him interested in grassroots communities. They can spark new life in any parish.

3. Consider joining one of the following groups devoted to justice and peace:

Amnesty International — an organization working for human rights mainly through letter-writing campaigns on behalf of people imprisoned around the world (especially those who are being tortured or are under the death penalty) because of their religious or political beliefs and who have not used violence to achieve their goals. In the United States: 304 W. 58th Street, New York, NY 10019. In Canada: 294 Albert Street, Suite 204, Ottawa, Ontario K1P 6E6.

Bread for the World — a ''gospel-centered and Christ-centered'' organization working to influence U.S. government policy on hunger issues. BFW organizes letter-writing campaigns and organizes educational seminars based usually in local churches. 6411 Chillum Place, N.W., Washington, D.C. 20012.

Clergy and Laity Concerned — an interfaith organization that works for the poor and oppressed by educating, organizing, and mobilizing the religious community around various peace and justice issues. CALC sponsors local and national events, produces educational materials, and promotes grassroots organizing. 198 Broadway, New York, NY 10038.

Pax Christi — the international movement of Catholics and others of good will devoted to a Gospel vision of peace, justice, and nonviolence. For the location of the group nearest you, contact: Pax Christi USA, 6337 W. Cornelia Avenue, Chicago, IL 60634; phone 312/736-2113.

4. When you read news articles about the Latin American struggle for justice, remember: these small Christian communities are the starting point for much of what is happening. See if that doesn't change your view of the events taking place. Too often we write off Latin American revolutions as the work of Communists or terrorists or both. Sometimes such people are involved, but the largest and most dynamic force in Latin America today consists of the thousands upon thousands of grassroots Christian communities. Your brothers and sisters are making a difference in their lives and their societies. Thousands of them — including priests and Sisters and bishops — have been persecuted and put to death for their faith.

They are a challenge to us all.

Points for Discussion

1. Pages 40-42 describe a grassroots Christian community in Latin America. In the North American Church, there are thousands of

similar communities — for example, peace and justice groups. Tell what you know of such groups in your general area.

2. Pages 42-46 give basic characteristics of a Latin American grass-roots Christian community. In forming such a group, which of these characteristics would you use as guidelines?

3. Would the Christian communities described in the New Testament (page 47) be labeled "Communist" if they existed today? Why or why not?

Recommended Reading

Developing Basic Christian Communities — A Handbook. Published by and available from: National Federation of Priests' Councils (NFPC), 1301 South Wabash Avenue, Chicago, IL 60605; phone 312/427-0115. $3.50.

Basic Christian Communities: The U.S. Experience. Published by and available from NFPC. $3.50. (This book is a companion volume to the above title. The price for the two, purchased together, is $6.50.)

Sergio Torres and John Eagleson, eds. *The Challenge of Basic Christian Communities*. Orbis Books, 1981. Paperback.

5
Communism and Capitalism: Does the Church Point to a Better Way?

Over the last twenty some years three popes — John XXIII, Paul VI, and John Paul II — have spoken forcefully on the social-political-economic realities of our times. They have been critical, to be sure, of the communist approach to these realities. But it may come as a surprise to many American Catholics that they have been critical of the capitalist approach as well.

In light of what we have said about justice and poverty, it is important at this point for us to review, even if briefly, what these three popes have said regarding communism and capitalism. For Christians involved in a very real world, as we are, the words of these popes are important. Theirs is a critical and prophetic stance: a challenge flowing from Christian values; a questioning of what many of us take for granted; a search for a better way. We may be tempted to refuse even to listen to what these popes have said. But it is most important that we remain open to their profoundly Christian reflections.

Statements of Earlier Popes

The three recent popes whom we are considering here stand in a long tradition of papal socioeconomic teaching. It will be helpful for us to review the basic elements of that teaching. (In Pope John XXIII's encyclical letter *Mater et Magistra,* by the way, we find one of the best summaries of what earlier popes have written concerning communism and capitalism; read paragraphs 10 through 45 of that document.)

Rerum Novarum. Leo XIII is given credit for being the first pope to face the modern world in an evaluative way. Leo was not all that comfortable with the new economic system of his day, which he and later popes referred to as *liberal capitalism.* In *Rerum Novarum* (published in 1891) the condition of workers especially bothered Leo. Work, he said, must not "be regarded as a mere commodity." The worker must be paid "according to the laws of justice and equity." Long before unions were popular he "affirmed the natural right (of workers) to enter corporately into associations" to establish and protect their rights.

Private property, which liberal capitalism considered an absolute right, was, he said, only a conditional right. "Private property, including that of productive goods, is a natural right possessed by all," but "he who uses (this) right . . . must take into account not merely his own welfare but that of others as well." Liberal capitalism was, in Leo's time, already exhibiting a marked antithesis to government intervention in the economy. Leo was clearly at odds with this as well. "The State, whose purpose is the realization of the common good in the temporal order, can by no means disregard the economic activity of its citizens." It must safeguard the rights of all its citizens, especially the weaker ones, and assure for them the "betterment of living conditions" and "a sufficient supply of material goods."

In summing up Leo's thought, John XXIII says that "unregulated competition which so-called *liberals* espouse, or the class struggle in the *Marxist sense,* are utterly opposed to Christian teaching and also to the very nature of man" (*Mater et Magistra,* 23). Both systems come in for their share of criticism.

Quadragesimo Anno. Forty years after the death of Leo XIII, Pope Pius XI returned to Leo's thought regarding the economic order. In his 1931 encyclical *Quadragesimo Anno* Pius XI reaffirmed the natural law character of private property. Yet he stressed "the social character and function of private ownership." He criticized the inhuman and unjust forms the wage system had taken and called for partnership arrangements so that "workers and officials (might) become partners in ownership, or management, or share in some manner in profits."

In 1931, what especially concerned Pius XI was that "economic power (had) been substituted for the free marketplace." He obviously was not at ease with the great barons of industry and the system of injustice they had created. The control that the wealthy and monopoly interests held over the economy was especially evil. This "unbridled ambition" for economic domination was bringing about new and increased suffering among workers and the poor. No just economic system, he insisted, could be built on special interests, unregulated competition, excessive power on the part of the wealthy, or vain nationalism. In one swift stroke he condemned all the sacred cows of the existing capitalist system of his day. What was necessary, he said, is that societies be run according to a juridical order that protects the common good of all.

Pope Pius XI took a strong stand against communism and the socioeconomic teachings of socialism; he was at pains to show how both were opposed to the teaching of the Church. We in the West are familiar with these teachings and to a large extent have espoused them. It is striking, however, that we seem hardly to have noticed his critical comments on liberal capitalism. It is fair to say, I believe, that many of us have heard only what we wanted to hear.

Pope John XXIII (1958-1963)

Pope John XXIII began this modern period of social comment with the encyclical letter *Mater et Magistra* in 1961. After his summary of what earlier popes had said, he went on to make his own observations. His comments fall mainly into two categories: (1) the workings of the economy itself, and (2) a serious problem he saw looming on the horizon.

The economy. In this first category, John singled out three economic factors which deserved special mention:

First, *workers* must have "some share in the enterprise, especially where they are paid no more than the minimum wage." He agreed with Pope Pius II that national wealth which is produced by all must benefit all and ensure the economic prosperity of all the people. For a wealthy owning class to "arrogate to itself what is produced" is completely unjust. Therefore, workers must "gradually acquire some share in the enterprise by such methods as seem . . . appropriate" (*Mater et Magistra,* 75, 76, 77).

Second, *private property* is a means by which human freedom is guaranteed. In those countries where private property is denied, the rights of individual citizens are jeopardized. People have the right to private possession of goods "including those of a productive kind." The means of production (capital, natural resources, factories) must not be controlled by one class over another: " . . . a continuing effort (must be) made to spread the use of this right through all ranks of the citizenry" (*Mater et Magistra,* 108 and 113).

Third, *governments* have an important role to play in economic affairs. Accordingly, the Pope says, "it is necessary that public authorities take active interest, the better to increase output of goods and to further social progress for the benefit of all citizens" (*Mater et Magistra,* 52).

By now, the state's obligation to assure the common good — over the particular good of individuals or of the owning class — has become an established canon of papal socioeconomic thought. Pope John amplifies this point by giving a long and thorough description of the tasks of public authority. It should reduce imbalances in the society, assure individual freedom, suitably regulate and foster individual and group freedom, provide principal services and social security, protect prices, and raise taxes for a just and equitable distribution of the wealth, etc.

Not surprisingly, these prescriptions angered the liberal capitalists (who, in the United States, are called "conservatives"). One conservative magazine entitled its response to this encyclical "Mater Si, Magistra No": the Church is Mother, but not Teacher. The fact that the letter also challenged socialist governments to grant greater freedom was, of course, applauded.

A serious problem. The problem Pope John saw looming on the horizon has since become an issue of great explosiveness and concern — the specter of Third World underdevelopment. "Our heart is filled with profound sadness," he wrote, "when we observe . . . great masses of workers, who, in not a few nations, and even in whole continents, receive too small a return from their labor." The sight of the "extreme need of the majority" pitted against the "wealth and conspicuous consumption of the few" called forth a stern judgment. While great strides had been made in modern society, "many nations . . . have not made identical progress in their economic and social affairs." He demanded aid to the less developed areas "to minimize the imbalance." But it must be, he said, help that does not seek to dominate, thus producing a new form of colonialism. He called this "the most pressing question of our day — the relationship between economically advanced commonwealths and those that are in the process of development" (*Mater et Magistra,* 68, 69, 122, 157). Pope John's successors to the chair of Peter have continued to deal with this still unresolved problem.

In his long ode to peace, the encyclical letter *Pacem in Terris* (1963), Pope John repeated the themes he had emphasized in *Mater et Magistra.* Here again, he insists that government recognize its duty to see to the common good of all the citizens and "safeguard the inviolable rights of the human person." These rights he describes in a list that includes the right to a worthy standard of living, moral and cultural rights, the rights to worship and to choose one's state in life, economic and political rights. He comes down hard on governments which deny personal freedom and spiritual values, an obvious reference to the communist governments.

Turning his attention to the underdeveloped countries, Pope John demands that the wealthy, more powerful nations respect the smaller, less powerful ones. In this encyclical letter he goes much further than before in noting the necessary interdependence of nations and in seeing the need for world government. The Pope lauds the United Nations and its efforts to uphold human rights. But he calls for a global public authority that can promote "the objective requirements of the universal common good." Today, the Pope says, "the universal common good poses problems of worldwide dimensions which cannot be adequately tackled or solved except by the efforts of public authorities endowed with a breadth of powers, structure and means of the same proportions: that is, of public authorities which are in a position to act in an effective manner on a worldwide basis. The moral order itself, therefore, demands that such a form of public authority be established.'' (See *Pacem in Terris,* 130 through 141.)

There was enough in all this to make both communists and capitalists sit up and take note!

Pope Paul VI (1963-1978)

Pope John's successor was very different from the outgoing and affectionate John XXIII. Paul VI was a quiet, retiring, brilliant man who quickly took up the challenge of global economic and social problems. A major encyclical, *Populorum Progressio* (1967), focused on the plight of underdeveloped nations. In this document Paul VI coined the now famous dictum, ''The new word for peace is development.'' World peace would come about only as a result of eliminating injustice.

Populorum Progressio. In this letter the Pope closely examines some of the basic tenets of capitalism and finds them seriously defective. He says: '' . . . it is unfortunate that on these new conditions of society a system has been constructed which considers *profit* as the key motive for economic progress, *competition* as the supreme law of economics, and *private ownership* of the means of production as an absolute right that has no limits and carries no corresponding social obligation. This unchecked liberalism leads to dictatorship, rightly denounced by Pius XI as producing 'the international imperialism of money.' One cannot condemn such abuses too strongly by solemnly recalling once again that the economy is at the service of man. . . . *capitalism* has been the cause of excessive *suffering, injustices,* and *fratricidal conflicts* whose effects still persist'' (*Populorum Progressio,* 26 — emphasis added).

There should be little doubt as to where Paul VI stands in regard to much of the ''conventional wisdom'' we hear from various leaders in business and government. But almost as if his condemnation of the main tenets of Western capitalist philosophy were not strong enough or sweeping enough, Pope Paul goes on to discuss several points in greater detail. He quotes Saint Ambrose, who says to the rich: "You are not making a gift of your possessions to the poor person. You are handing over to him what is his. For what has been given in common for the use of all, you have arrogated to yourself. The world is given to all, and not only to the rich." Pope Paul then adds, "That is, private property does not constitute for anyone an absolute and unconditioned right. No one is justified in keeping for his exclusive use what he does not need, when others lack necessities." At times the common good, he says, even demands expropriation. (*Populorum Progressio,* 23 and 24)

Paul VI is no less severe with another tenet of liberal capitalism, the notion of "free trade." Highly industrialized nations benefit from this so-called free system to the detriment of poorer nations. "The poor nations," he says, "remain ever poor while the rich ones become still richer." He concludes, " . . . the rule of free trade, taken by itself, is no longer able to govern international relations. . . . The situation is no longer the same when economic conditions differ too widely from country to country: prices which are 'freely' set in the market can produce unfair results. One must recognize that it is the fundamental principle of liberalism, as a rule for commercial exchange, which is questioned here" (*Populorum Progressio,* 57 and 58).

Octagesima Adveniens. One of the great "sleepers" among papal socioeconomic statements is another letter of Paul VI, *Octagesima Adveniens* (1971), written on the eightieth anniversary of Leo XIII's *Rerum Novarum. Octagesima Adveniens* squarely faces the two dominant ideological systems of the day. In categorical terms the Pope states:

" . . . *the Christian who wishes to live his faith in a political activity which he thinks of as service cannot, without contradicting himself, adhere to ideological systems which radically or sub-*

stantially go against his faith and his concept of man. He cannot adhere to the Marxist ideology, to its atheistic materialism, to its dialectic of violence and to the way it absorbs individual freedom in the collectivity, at the same time denying all transcendence to man and his personal and collective history; nor can he adhere to the liberal ideology which believes it exalts individual freedom by withdrawing it from every limitation, by stimulating it through exclusive seeking of interest and power, and by considering social solidarities as more or less automatic consequences of individual initiatives, not as an aim and a major criterion of the value of the social organization" (Octagesima Adveniens, 26).

Both systems, in short, have serious drawbacks. One system represses human freedom in the collectivity to the point of denying man's spiritual nature and his openness to the Divine; the other system canonizes human freedom into a cult that has no regard for the common good or for human community.

Later, in paragraph 31 of the same letter, Pope Paul does something of note. He pursues the question of distinguishing various levels of Marxism which John XXIII had raised. Pope Paul is aware that many Christians today are drawn to various developments of socialism. They recognize that it is different in different places. Nonetheless, he says, it should not be idealized, for the various historical forms of Marxism always remain "conditioned by the ideologies from which they originated."

What are the various levels of Marxism as perceived by Paul VI? They number four:

Level 1 — the active practice of class struggle;

Level 2 — the collective exercise of political and economic power under the direction of a single party;

Level 3 — a socialist ideology based on historical materialism and the denial of everything transcendent;

Level 4 — a rigorous method of examining social and political reality and the practice of revolutionary transformation.

The first three levels of Marxism are clearly unacceptable to the Christian, denying as they do, in turn: the common brotherhood of mankind (Level 1); the freedom of the human person (Level 2); and the spiritual and religious nature of man (Level 3). While the fourth level may be open for consideration, the Christian must still not forget the ideology which binds the four levels together and leads to a totalitarian and violent society. This, Pope Paul says, calls for careful discernment.

The Pope then goes on to refer again to the erroneous affirmation of individual freedom which is the ideology underlying liberal capitalism. This, he says, calls for no less careful discernment. Elsewhere in this letter he singles out the multinational corporations, which have become a law unto themselves, and the danger they are to the world economy. They are, he says, "largely independent of the national political powers and therefore not subject to control from the point of view of the common good. . . . these private organizations can lead to a new and abusive form of economic domination . . . " (*Octagesima Adveniens,* 35 and 44). What Pius XI feared in the presence of monopoly power, Paul VI sees happening in the multinational corporations.

Pope John Paul II (1978-   )

John Paul II began his pontificate with a long, personalistic letter entitled *Redemptor Hominis* (1979). While not dealing directly with the economic order, this encyclical makes two very important observations on it.

Redemptor Hominis. First, the Pope points to "the picture of a consumer civilization, which consists in a certain surplus of goods necessary for man and for entire societies — and we are dealing precisely with the rich, highly developed societies — while the remaining societies — at least broad sectors of them — are suffering from hunger, with many people dying each day of starvation and malnutrition" (*Redemptor Hominis,* 16).

This vast division the Pope sees as an abuse of freedom by one group which concomitantly limits the freedom of the others. One group of people, living in freedom and having much, dominates another group of people who are deprived of the little they have. This drama of rich and poor, as he calls it, is made even worse by the presence of "privileged social classes and of the rich countries, which accumulate goods to an excessive degree and the misuse of whose riches very often becomes the cause of various ills" (*Redemptor Hominis,* 16).

The second evil the Pope points to in this encyclical is the presence of "totalitarianisms." The plural is interesting — the inference being that totalitarianism is not limited to one kind of political system, but exists wherever, as he defines it, there is "the imposition of power by a certain group upon all the other members of the society." (One thinks here, of course, not only of Communist eastern bloc countries but of the many military dictatorships in Latin America.) These totalitarian governments contradict the very essence of the state which "as a political community, consists in that the society and people composing it are master and sovereign of their own destiny" (*Redemptor Hominis,* 17).

So widespread is the problem of rich and poor, of the free and the dominated, "that it brings into question the financial, monetary, production and commercial mechanisms that, resting on various political pressures, support the world economy." Both systems — capitalism and communism, in other words — "are proving incapable either of remedying unjust social situations . . . or of dealing with the urgent challenges and ethical demands of the present" (*Redemptor Hominis,* 16). The Pope's reflection on the issue stops at this point in *Redemptor Hominis*. He resumes his line of thought with all seriousness in his next great letter on the socioeconomic situation, *On Human Work,* published in 1981.

On Human Work. The beginning point for John Paul's comment on human work is man the worker. All else — the economic and political systems of capitalism and communism — must be at the service of the worker. The great principle laid down in the letter is "the principle of the priority of labor over capital." Capital belongs to labor. It "cannot be separated from labor" (*On Human Work,* 12 and 13).

John Paul sees this foundation as thoroughly and deeply biblical. To his earliest creation God says in Genesis, "Be fruitful and multiply, and fill the earth and subdue it." John Paul takes great pains to show that both systems, capitalism and communism, violate this fundamental principle of the working world.

Both systems have *separated labor from capital.* In each, control over capital, which rightly belongs to the worker, has passed to someone else. In the capitalist economies, work is treated as a kind of merchandise which the worker sells to the employer. The employer has taken control over capital. In collective economies, on the other hand, the worker is upheld in theory as a dominant part of the economic system. But in actual fact, control over capital has passed from the worker to the state. In each system, the worker is left bereft of what is rightfully his. A group — either the owning class or the ruling class — has taken hold of capital and turned it against the worker.

The "fundamental error" in this structuring of the world of work is what John Paul II calls "economism." It is a kind of *materialism* that places the spiritual and the personal "in a position of subordination to material reality." Both capitalism and collectivism do this. For capitalism, it is a practical rather than a theoretical materialism. Capitalism began by subordinating labor to capital, by separating labor and capital in the practical order. The person of the worker was effectively ignored in early liberal capitalism, as it is today in many Third World countries.

In opposition to this unjust economistic materialism, that treated the worker as a mere cog in the wheel of production, arose dialectical materialism. This is the theoretical materialism that underlies the collectivist system. It intends to counteract the first materialism by giving a rationale to "the separation of labor and capital" that already existed by "setting them up in opposition as two production factors." But it falls into the same trap as capitalistic materialism. "In dialectical materialism too man is not first and foremost the subject of work and the efficient cause of the productive process" (*On Human Work,* 13).

Capitalism and communism fail in still another way. Each of them is in conflict with the Church's teaching on ownership of *private property.* The collectivism of Marxism is clearly at odds with this teaching in its denial of private ownership. But liberal capitalist practice is also opposed insofar as "Christian tradition has never upheld this right as absolute and untouchable" as liberal capitalism does. "The right to private property is subordinated to the right to common use, to the fact that goods are meant for everyone." The capitalist practice of allowing a wealthy owning class to have practically no restrictions on their wealth is an outrage against the Church's stated position of "the right common to all to use the goods of the whole creation."

In addition, the principle of the priority of labor over capital in *On Human Work* stresses another aspect of ownership — the right of workers to own the *means of production.* The Pope states that " . . . property is acquired first of all through work in order that it may serve work." The means of production "cannot be possessed against labor, they cannot even be possessed for possession's sake. . . . " Yet in both capitalist and collectivist economies, the means of production (capital) are possessed against labor. In capitalist economies, they are possessed by the owning class — for example, the oligarchies of El Salvador and Guatemala. In collectivist economies, they are possessed by the state — for example, in Poland.

To change this state of affairs, John Paul II calls for a new *socialization* of the means of production by which workers would come to control capital. This new socialization would lie between the capitalist and collectivist systems. It might include such things as "joint ownership of the means of work, sharing by the workers in the management and/or profits of businesses, so-called shareholding by labor, etc." In these ways capitalism would be revised to be more in line with human rights and Christian teaching. John Paul expressly rejects the "*a priori* elimination of private ownership of the means of production" as practiced in collectivist states. This, he says, "is not enough to ensure their satisfactory socialization" because the means of production merely pass to the control of those who run the government, not to the workers; " . . . merely converting the means of production into state property in the collectivist systems is by no means equivalent to 'socializing' that property" (*On Human Work,* 14).

Though state collectivism is not an answer, John Paul II gives great weight to the legitimate role of government in the economy. He ascribes to this "indirect employer," as he calls government, a list of economic responsibilities that any reader of the encyclicals is by now familiar with. Topping this list, in what he calls its primary function, is the state's responsibility to ensure "suitable employment for all who are capable of it" (*On Human Work,* 18).

In this letter John Paul speaks of solidarity. Its Polish overtones are unmistakable. Workers must be allowed — in solidarity with one another — to pursue the goal of taking priority over capital. Their right to association is vigorously asserted. He states that "there is a need for ever new movements of solidarity of the workers and with the workers. This solidarity must be present whenever it is called for by the social degrading of the subject of work, by exploitation of the workers and by the growing areas of poverty and even hunger" (*On Human Work,* 8).

One knows how much the heart of this Polish pope must have been with his countrymen in their struggle against oppression as he wrote this letter. But John Paul makes it clear that he recognizes many other forms of oppression as well. In his letters, as in the writing of other recent popes, both liberal capitalism and Marxist collectivism stand censured.

Conclusion

We live in a world, as John Paul II emphasizes, in which two political economic systems are dominant. Neither has radically changed. Capitalism has made some cosmetic corrections to better the conditions of its workers. But it is still subject to the control of wealthy owning elites and powerful — now multinational — corporations. Despite taxation, there remains a private property structure that has not lessened the gap between enormous wealth and incredible poverty. Workers, for the most part, have not been allowed to take their position of priority over capital. Governments still are too one-sidedly in support of the wealthy and the corporations and too weakly on the side of the poor and the powerless.

Communism still denies freedom to individuals through its system of collectivization and state control and through its professed materialism which shuts off access to what is truly human, spiritual, and religious.

We can say: "But our system is better than theirs." Yet, in doing so, we miss the point. Our system is not — and neither is theirs — good enough. Both together are responsible for increasing suffering in the present day. Both need radical change.

Points for Discussion

1. What do the popes find wrong with capitalism?
2. What do the popes find wrong with communism?
3. What do the popes see as the most pressing problem in today's world?
4. What solutions do the popes propose in the economic order? in the political order?

Recommended Reading

David J. O'Brien and Thomas A. Shannon, eds., *Renewing the Earth: Catholic Documents on Peace, Justice and Liberation.* Doubleday Image Books, 1977. Paperback.

Quest for Justice: A Compendium of the Statements of the United States Catholic Bishops on the Political and Social Order, 1966-1980. Office of Publishing Services, United States Catholic Conference. Catalog No. 649. $15.